Pre-reader

Hello, Penguin!

Kathryn Williams

NATIONAL GEOGRAPHIC

Washington, D.C.

Vocabulary Tree

ANIMALS

PENGUINS

WHERE THEY LIVE

on the ice
on the beach
in the forest

WHAT THEY DO

huddle
shuffle
slide
swim

WHAT THEY LOOK LIKE

big
small
fancy
plain

Hello, penguin!

It's cold! These penguins live on the ice.

emperor penguins

They huddle to keep warm.

There are many kinds of penguins.
This kind lives on the beach.

Magellanic penguins

They make nests in the
dirt and sand.

These penguins live in the forest!

Snares penguins

They waddle over tree roots.

Some kinds of penguins are big,

emperor penguin

and some are small.

fairy penguin

rockhopper penguin

Some are fancy,

Adélie penguin

and some are plain.

Penguins can't fly.
But they can shuffle.

chinstrap penguins

And they can slide!

They use their wings to swim.

Adélie penguins

Splash!

It's time to go fishing!

Humboldt penguin

This penguin gets
a yummy fish.

After a swim, it's time to go back on land.

gentoo penguins

Hello, penguin!

KINDS OF PENGUINS

There are many kinds of penguins.
These are the kinds in this book.

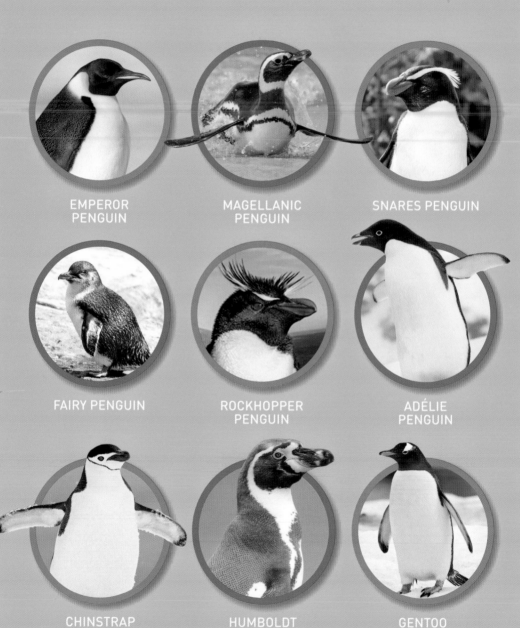

EMPEROR
PENGUIN

MAGELLANIC
PENGUIN

SNARES PENGUIN

FAIRY PENGUIN

ROCKHOPPER
PENGUIN

ADÉLIE
PENGUIN

CHINSTRAP
PENGUIN

HUMBOLDT
PENGUIN

GENTOO
PENGUIN

YOUR TURN!

Draw a penguin. Now tell a story about your penguin. Where does it live? What does it do?

For my mom —K.M.W.

The author and publisher gratefully acknowledge the expert content review of this book by Darwin Long, senior aviculturist at the Audubon Aquarium of the Americas, and the literacy review of this book by Kimberly Gillow, principal, Milan Area Schools, Michigan.

Published by National Geographic Partners, LLC, Washington, D.C. 20036. All rights reserved. Reproduction in whole or in part without written permission of the publisher is prohibited.

NATIONAL GEOGRAPHIC and Yellow Border Design are trademarks of the National Geographic Society, used under license.

Designed by Sanjida Rashid

Library of Congress Cataloging-in-Publication Data
Names: Williams, Kathryn (Kathryn Marie), author.
Title: Hello, penguin! / by Kathryn Williams.
Description: Washington, D.C. : National Geographic Kids, [2017] | Series: National geographic reader | Audience: Age 2-5. | Audience: Pre-school, excluding Grade K. |
Identifiers: LCCN 2017010742 (print) | LCCN 2017011788 (ebook) | ISBN 9781426328978 (e-book) | ISBN 9781426328985 (e-book + audio) | ISBN 9781426328954 (pbk. : alk. paper) | ISBN 9781426328961 (hardcover : alk. paper)
Subjects: LCSH: Penguins--Juvenile literature.
Classification: LCC QL696.S473 (ebook) | LCC QL696. S473 W49 2017 (print) | DDC 598.47--dc23
LC record available at https://lccn.loc.gov/2017010742

Photo Credits
GI = Getty Images, MP = Minden Pictures
Cover, Andy Rouse/MP; 1 , Tom Walker/GI; 2-3, Jan Vermeer/MP; 4, Tui De Roy/MP; 5, Mint Images–Frans Lanting/GI; 6, Alain Mafart–Renodier/Biosphoto/MP; 7, Buenaventuramariano/GI; 8, Ole Jorgen Liodden/NPL/MP; 9, Tui De Roy/MP; 10, Martin Ruegner/GI; 11, Shannon Hibberd/National Geographic Creative; 12, Rhinie van Meurs/NIS/MP; 13, Patrick J. Endres/GI; 14, Ralph Lee Hopkins/National Geographic Creative; 15, Flip Nicklin/MP; 16–17, Patrick J. Endres/GI; 18–19, Gerard Lacz/Visuals Unlimited, Inc./GI; 20, Momatiuk–Eastcott/GI; 21, Brian J. Skerry/National Geographic Creative; 22 (UP LE), Thorsten Milse/robertharding/GI; 22 (UP CTR), Patrick J. Endres/GI; 22 (UP RT), Tui De Roy/MP; 22 (CTR LE), Olga Khoroshunova/Alamy; 22 (CTR), Glenn Bartley/BIA/MP/GI; 22 (CTR RT), Bryan and Cherry Alexander/Nature Picture Library; 22 (LO LE), Ira Meyer/National Geographic Creative; 22 (LO CTR), Cyril Ruoso/MP; 22 (LO RT), Greg Smith/National Geographic My Shot; 23 (UP RT), bogdan ionescu/Shutterstock; 23 (CTR), Peyton Larsen 23 (LO LE), Lukas Gojda/Shutterstock

National Geographic supports K–12 educators with ELA Common Core Resources. Visit natgeoed.org /commoncore for more information.

Printed in the United States of America
22/WOR/5